FAIRIES

raintree
a Capstone company — publishers for children

Raintree is an imprint of Capstone Global Library Limited, a company incorporated in England and Wales having its registered office at 264 Banbury Road, Oxford, OX2 7DY – Registered company number: 6695582

www.raintree.co.uk
myorders@raintree.co.uk

Hardback edition © Capstone Global Library Limited 2022
Paperback edition © Capstone Global Library Limited 2023
The moral rights of the proprietor have been asserted.

All rights reserved. No part of this publication may be reproduced in any form or by any means (including photocopying or storing it in any medium by electronic means and whether or not transiently or incidentally to some other use of this publication) without the written permission of the copyright owner, except in accordance with the provisions of the Copyright, Designs and Patents Act 1988 or under the terms of a licence issued by the Copyright Licensing Agency, 5th Floor, Shackleton House, 4 Battle Bridge Lane, London SE1 2HX (www.cla.co.uk). Applications for the copyright owner's written permission should be addressed to the publisher.

Editor: Julie Gassman
Designer: Hilary Wacholz

Original illustrations © Capstone Global Library Limited 2020
Originated by Capstone Global Library Ltd

ISBN 978 1 3982 3523 6 (hardback)
ISBN 978 1 3982 3524 3 (paperback)

British Library Cataloguing in Publication Data
A full catalogue record for this book is available from the British Library.

All the internet addresses (URLs) given in this book were valid at the time of going to press. However, due to the dynamic nature of the internet, some addresses may have changed, or sites may have changed or ceased to exist since publication. While the author and publisher regret any inconvenience this may cause readers, no responsibility for any such changes can be accepted by either the author or the publisher.

Printed and bound in India.

FAIRIES

by Suma Subramaniam

illustrated by Martín Bustamante

It's a warm day in the village. Everyone is going about their work. Everything is the same as usual. But then you see a faint light. You follow it and notice wings.

Before you can catch a glimpse, the creature disappears in a flash. You wonder what it could be. A bird? A dragonfly?

Or maybe it is something more magical . . . a fairy, perhaps?

WHAT IS A FAIRY?

A fairy is a mythical creature who looks like a human, often with wings. The word fairy comes from the Latin word *fata*, or spirit. It is also sometimes spelt "faerie", which is an old French spelling. Fairies can be female or male. Some people say that fairies don't exist. But fairies have lived with us in stories for a long time.

FAIRY BEHAVIOUR

Because fairies are magical, they have endless abilities. They can fly through the sky. They can tumble deep down underground. They can swim in seas. They can sparkle in light.

Fairies can change their size and shape. They can be smaller than your thumb, taller than a giant Redwood tree or everything in between. They can be quite beautiful or quite ugly. They appear the way they want to be seen.

Fairies can be good or bad. Good fairies help people in need. They make rainbows and flowers. They change the colours of the leaves in autumn. They weave magic into herbs to increase their healing powers.

Bad fairies kidnap women and carry children away to fairyland. They keep them hidden from everyone.

Fairies live among humans. But humans cannot see them unless the fairies want to be seen. Look inside caves. Check amongst the roots of forest trees. You may even find them in your garden. But be quick! They will disappear in the blink of an eye.

There are five elements – air, earth, water, fire and space – that make up our world. Fairies live in any of these elements. They protect plants, take care of animals, hide in the clouds and guard bodies of water.

LIFE CYCLE OF A FAIRY

Fairies go through many changes as they grow. They can live forever.

FLUTTERPILLAR

After a few weeks, a flutterpillar hatches from the egg. The fairy mother feeds her newborn with milk.

FAIRY EGG

A fairy lays one or two eggs on a leaf or a twig. The eggs are like tiny butterfly eggs and are covered in beautiful patterns.

COCOON

After many months, the flutterpillar's parents make a cocoon out of leaves, petals or spider's silk. Then a winged fairy called a moppet emerges from the cocoon.

MOPPET

The moppet is still a baby and needs its parents' care until it is fully grown at three years old.

FAIRY FEATURES

BONES
A fairy's bones are hollow. They are filled with air pockets that look like a honeycomb.

COLLARBONE
A fairy has a fused collarbone like a bird. It is called a wishbone and it helps her fly.

WINGS
Many fairies have four wings – two on each side. The wings reflect light, which makes them sparkle.

FEET
A fairy that lives on land has toes like a human. A fairy that lives in water has webbed feet.

EARS
Fairy ears are pointed.

MUSCLES
A fairy has lots of small, strong chest muscles that help her move her wings. She has an extra set of flight muscles running down the middle of her back.

TYPES OF FAIRIES

Sprite fairies are small, supernatural beings. Some make their homes high up in trees. Others live in water. Sprite fairies travel in swarms, and they can bite if you upset them.

SPRITE FAIRIES

Sylph fairies look like clouds. They help humans with their problems by helping them think clearly.

Nymphs live among rivers, seas, trees, meadows and mountains. They appear as young, beautiful, gentle girls. Nymphs are often honoured for their creative powers.

Apsaras are a type of nymph. They are singers and dancers who perform at the courts of gods. They live in water, clouds and the heavens. Because apsaras do not have wings, their wavy clothes help them fly.

APSARAS

GOBLINS

Goblins are evil, mischievous and ugly fairies that live in caves and other dark places. They frighten children and make trouble. Goblins are always dangerous to human beings.

ELVES

Elves come from German mythology and English folklore. They appear as small nature spirits or beautiful young men and women. These friendly, kind fairies live in forests, under the ground or in wells and springs.

Pixies are tiny fairies that rest under mushrooms. They fly with lovely butterfly or dragonfly wings, and some have blue or green skin. They protect flowers and horses and can charm humans into joining their dancing.

PIXIE

Brownies are helpful fairies. They live in human homes where they do useful work. They like to keep homes clean every day.

BROWNIE

TOOTH FAIRY

When a baby tooth falls out, you put it under your pillow at bedtime and hope for a visit from a tooth fairy. A tooth fairy collects and uses the teeth to build her castle. In return, she leaves you a gift.

Fairy godmothers have magical powers. They make good things happen to you as long as you believe in them.

FAIRY GODMOTHER

Fairies hold the promise of creating wonder and beauty for humans to enjoy.

Step outside and look closely at the nature surrounding you.
Perhaps a fairy will appear to cast some magic and surprise you.

ABOUT THE AUTHOR

Suma Subramaniam is the contributing author of *The Hero Next Door*. She is also the author of *Fairies, She Sang for India: How M.S. Subbulakshmi Used Her Voice for Change*, and *Namaste Is a Greeting*. She hires software professionals during the day and is a writer by night. Suma has degrees in creative writing and in computer science and management. Visit her website at sumasubramaniam.com.

ABOUT THE ILLUSTRATOR

Martín Bustamante is an illustrator and painter from Argentina. At the age of three, he was able to draw a horse "starting by the tail", as his mother always says. As a teenager, he found new and fascinating worlds full of colours, shapes and atmospheres in films such as *Star Wars* and books like *Prince Valiant*, by Harold Foster, and these became his inspiration for drawing. He started working as a professional illustrator and has worked for several editorials and magazines, from Argentina to the United States to Europe.

GLOSSARY

being living thing

element one of five substances (earth, water, fire, air and space) that some people believe make up everything in nature

folklore tales, sayings and customs among a group of people

glimpse brief look

mischievous able or tending to cause trouble in a playful way

mythical based on stories from ancient times

supernatural something that cannot be given an ordinary explanation

COMPREHENSION QUESTIONS

1. Based on what you've read, do you think most fairies are good or bad? Explain your answer.

2. Review the various types of fairies on pages 18–25. Which type of fairy would you most like to meet? Why? Which would you least like to meet?

3. Fairies can decide how they want to appear. If you were a fairy, how would you appear? Write a paragraph and draw a picture.

FIND OUT MORE

BOOKS

A Natural History of Fairies (Folklore Field Guides), Emily Hawkins (Frances Lincoln Children's Books, 2020)

Discover Gnomes, Halflings and Other Wondrous Fantasy Beings (All About Fantasy Creatures), Aaron J. Sautter (Raintree, 2018)

The Book of Mythical Beasts and Magical Creatures, Stephen Krensky (DK Children, 2020)

WEBSITES

brushbaby.com/blogs/news/national-tooth-fairy-day
Find out some fun facts about the tooth fairy.

woodlandtrust.org.uk/blog/2019/04/how-to-make-fairy-doors/
Learn how to make a fairy door and other fun fairy activities with the Woodland Trust.

READ THEM ALL!

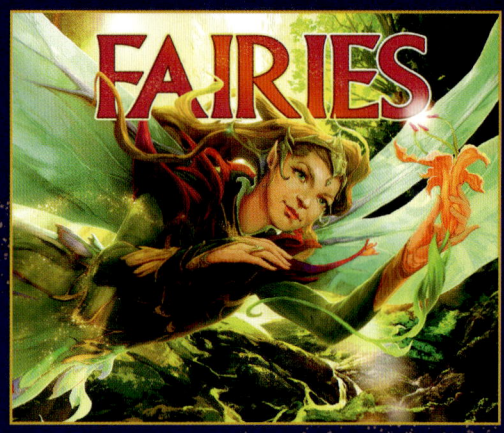
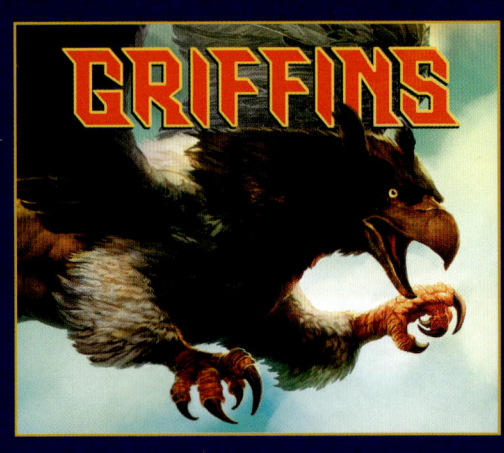

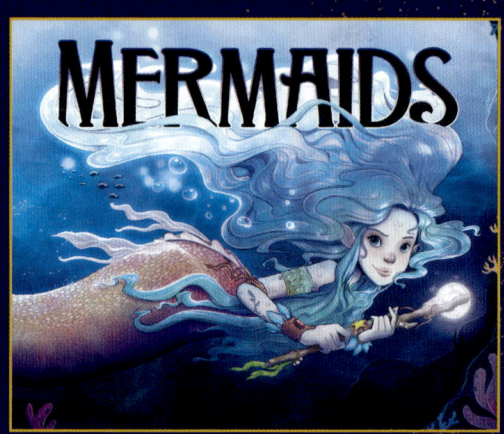